Beyond The Anthropocene Epoch

Sharon Leontine Wallenberg

Liberty 16 Books, Inc.

Library of Congress

ISBN: 979-8-9882618-6-5

Published by: Liberty 61 Books

www.Liberty61Books.com

Dedication

This book is dedicated to the Creator of our beloved home planet Earth, and to the hope that planet Earth is moving from the Bible's Garden of Eden described in Genesis to the Peaceful Kingdom described in Isaiah:

Beyond the Anthropocene Epoch.

Introduction

The Anthropocene Epoch is an unofficial unit of geological time describing the most recent period in earth's history. The Anthropocene Epoch started about 200 years ago and includes the world today. The Anthropocene Epoch is characterized by the human species having a significant impact on the planet's climate and ecosystems, and most importantly, on other species.

During the Anthropocene Epoch the human species has become the single most influential and powerful species on the planet. Lack of human responsibility and concern has caused significant changes on planet Earth including global warming, species extinction, zoonotic pandemics, pollution of land, water and air, changes to land including desertification and deforestation, many other environment issues, including pollution and warming of the atmosphere.

Human society has become so powerful that it affects the fate of the entire biosphere. Unfortunately, this paradigm shift in influence has not been accompanied by the necessary responsibility, foresight, accountability, or justice, to create and maintain sustainability. These values contrast sharply with the prevailing logic of profitability as the raison d'être for our current growth-based economic system.

This book attempts to shed light on these issues and hopes to facilitate movement Beyond the Anthropocene Epoch.

Contents

The facts and ideas presented here are like flowers, and I am the ribbon holding them all together.

Part One: The Problem: Speciesism

Part Three: The Solution: Legislation

Part One

The Problem: Speciesism

1 The World Health Summit

The World Health Summit held in Berlin, October 2022, was the leading international annual meeting for global health. Jointly organized with the United Nations World Health Organization (WHO), the three-day Conference involved 61 Panel Discussions, 404 Speakers, more than 200 Women Speakers, and more than 200 Men Speakers. It attracted over 4,100 participants from over 140 nations, including more than 30 Government Ministers from around the world. and an additional 60,000 individuals who participated virtually.

"This year the World Health Summit is focusing particularly on the complex interdependency between climate change, food systems, digital transformation, peace and global health," according to Olaf Scholtz, Chancellor of the Federal Republic of Germany at the Opening Ceremony of the 2022 Berlin World Health Summit.

"We are united around one goal: to end the pandemic while developing more equitable and sustainable models", commented Emanuel Macron, President of the Republic of France at the Opening Ceremony of the 2022 Berlin World Health Summit.

Only one of all the Speakers at the World Health Summit mentioned the word "Justice". It was Marco Lambertini of the World Wildlife Fund International at the Closing Ceremony.

If more attention were paid to the simple concept of going beyond the Anthropocene Epoch, and incorporating Justice into the equation, this planet would not be in the unhealthy condition it is in now.

The World Health Summit focused on many topics, but missed the fact that almost all of the health issues discussed traced back to their Anthropocene roots, and the fact that almost all of these issues could be solved by moving past the Anthropocene epoch.

2

Pandemics: Hiding In Plain Sight

"Architecture for Pandemic Preparedness", was one of the panels at the Berlin World Health Summit. However, the simple and direct solution - eliminating speciesism - was never even mentioned.

Pandemics are the direct result of speciesism – the abuse, exploitation and destruction of other species for the supposed benefit of the human species. The results of speciesism are causing pandemics, destroying the planet with climate change, species extinction, loss of biodiversity, pollution of air, water, and land, misuse of scarce resources, and more.

Pandemics come with accompanying skyrocketing health care costs. The resulting economic burden is unsustainable in the developing nations. The simplest and most direct way to prepare for pandemics is to avoid them by eliminating speciesism. This was never mentioned at all the sophisticated and technical meetings of the Berlin World Health Summit.

According to the United Nations Summit on Biodiversity, the emergence of deadly zoonotic diseases (HIV/AIDS, Ebola, SARS, MERS, Spanish, Black, Swine and Avian Flu, Covid-19, and others) are the direct result of human imbalance with nature, specifically the supremacist exploitation of other species by humans. Emerging diseases and pandemics are almost invariably zoonotic. An estimated 60% of all viruses that infect humans came from animals, and 75% of all new infectious diseases in the past decade are zoonotic. The global rate of zoonotic disease is drastically increasing.

In the world today, the non-human population outnumbers human population by literally billions. This is not because of wild animal populations. Species extinction and habitat destruction are causing these individuals to quickly disappear. This gigantic difference in population is due to the individuals raised in the horrific conditions that breed disease and suffering - innocent animals raised and murdered for human food.

Under these circumstances, pathogens appear which threaten the lives, health, and incomes of the worldwide human population who eat innocent, exploited individuals and their menstrual cycles, also known as eggs, and drink the milk meant by nature for their own children, not for humans. According to the United Nations World Health Organization (WHO) the greatest contributing factors of pandemic disease is the way food (non-human individuals) are produced, and the misuse of antibiotics.

Zoonotic pandemics are inevitable, given the increasing incursion of human beings into wildlife habitat, usually to expand animal agriculture. 75% of earth's land areas have already been heavily transformed by human activity. Species are presently going extinct at approximately 1,000 times the natural rate.

Habitat destruction, biodiversity loss, and humanity's encroachment on wildlands increase the risk of zoonotic disease. Scientists agree that habitat loss is positively correlated with increased zoonotic pandemics. This is because high biodiversity reduces the risk of zoonotic disease by the 'Dilution Effect' and protects human health by reducing the risk of zoonotic disease. Habitat destruction facilitates pandemics.

As animal agriculture grows, more and more resources of land and water are needed, causing the destruction of the habitats of existing species, and causing extinction of unique and irreplaceable individuals. This loss of biodiversity is a main contributing factor fueling zoonotic pandemics.

There is no way to humanely and safely confine and exploit animals. This has not worked. The United Nations recommends stricter regulations of live markets. The United Nations Universal Declaration of Animal Welfare, and global investigations have not been effective in solving the problem. Neither have any local or national laws or ordinances. What is needed is a radical, comprehensive approach. The only effective way to prepare for pandemics is to eliminate speciesism, an idea that was never mentioned at the World Health Summit.

3

NCDs: Deadlier Than Pandemics

"From Words To Action For Better Non-Communicable Disease Outcomes." According to this Health Summit Panel, 'Non-Communicable Diseases (NCDs), including cardiovascular diseases, cancer, chronic obstructive pulmonary disease, and diabetes, as well as mental health disorders including suicide, are now the dominant cause of death and disability across the world.'

The panel mentioned 'research' and 'innovative approaches', and 'improved access to treatment', but not the proactive approach of adopting a plant-based diet, and eliminating meat, dairy (including cheese and yogurt), fish, and sea individuals. The meat, dairy and fish-based diet has been linked to the NCDs of heart disease, diabetes, obesity, and some cancers due to the overabundance of fat and cholesterol which is only present in sentient beings who are eaten for food, and are not found in plants.

Suicide is quickly becoming a leading cause of death worldwide according to the Summit. Depression and suicide are linked to the meat and dairy based diet. Cortisol is the main stress hormone present in both humans and animals in stressful situations. Slaughter, incarceration, a life of rape, kidnapped babies, and 'milking' which involves the human induced torture of stabbings in the eyes and other areas, tail breaking, kicking, beating, flame throwing at sensitive udders, lack of sanitation, involved in 'milking' docile childless mother cows are stressful. Cortisol from stress affects mood disorders, especially depression. Excessive amounts of cortisol are ingested by humans who eat animals and drink their milk. This excessive cortisol causes human depression, often resulting in suicide. Eating a sustainable, healthful plant-based diet can eliminate depression and possibility suicide.

Antimicrobial Resistance is a Global Challenge. AMR has caused an estimated 4.5 million deaths associated with bacteria in 2019, making it a leading cause of death worldwide.

The meat and dairy based diet is the main cause of antimicrobial resistance. Deadly AMR is caused by the enormous amounts of antibiotics forced on incarcerated animals. These excessive amounts of antibiotics are used to keep these unfortunate individuals from perishing prematurely due to the horrendous conditions in which they are forced to live, before a human profit can be made on their suffering. These excessive amounts of antibiotics are then consumed by the humans who eat the flesh and menstrual cycles (eggs) of these unfortunate individuals and drink the milk. This important, and possibly singular, causative factor was not explored in the panels.

4

Promoting Healthier Politics

"Investment for Health and Wellbeing" missed one of the most important financial aspects of health and wellbeing. According to many experts, the single most significant financial maneuver which would enhance human and planetary health and wellbeing is to end subsidies on sentient beings consumed by humans as food: meat, poultry, dairy and fish.

Government subsidies benefiting the food industry are responsible for negative effects on human health, specifically the Non-Communicable Diseases (NCDs) of heart disease, diabetes, obesity, AMR, some cancers in developed nations, and cause hunger, starvation, and poverty in the developing nations.

Government financial subsidies benefiting the meat and dairy industries keep prices artificially low on the unsustainable and unhealthful meat and dairy based diet, while causing human NCDs and the multiple negative effects on the planet including climate change, pollution of air, land, and water, species extinction, habitat destruction, deforestation, desertification, land degradation, and biodiversity loss. Most importantly, it causes the immense suffering of innocent sentient individuals.

Removing the financial political subsidies on exploiting sentient land animals and sea individuals would assure that humans who choose to consume unhealthful and unsustainable meat, dairy, fish and sea individuals would pay lower financial costs, thus incentivizing humans to make more healthful, planet friendly, humane food choices - ideally the healthful whole food plant-based diet which does not receive these politically motivated subsidies. This would have the additional financial benefit of reducing health care costs by eliminating the cause of most non-communicable diseases, diabetes, heart disease, some cancers, obesity and antimicrobial resistance.

According to Oxford University economic projections, "Removal of subsidy dependent animal flesh and secretions from the global food system could save over a trillion dollars in environmental costs in the next 30 years. The exorbitant health care costs related to the meat and dairy based diet caused non-communicable diseases, (NCDs), would be reduced or eliminated when alternatives plant-based diets are allowed to compete in a free market."

Eliminating political financial subsidies on sentient beings eaten as food would incentivize consumers in the developed nations to eat more sustainable and healthful plant-based foods, eliminating the need to purchase grain from the developing nations to feed to unjustly incarcerated individuals raised as human food. That grain can then be used to reduce or eliminate hunger, starvation and poverty in the nations forced to export their grain at subsidy related artificially low prices while they and their own children are hungry or starving.

Governments should eliminate subsidies to animal agriculture and instead support sustainable agriculture known by the following names: Veganic (North America), Stock-Free Organic (Europe), and Natural Farming Practices (India). These agricultural methods use no expensive and harmful fertilizers or pesticides. They maintain soil fertility naturally by plowing under nitrogen rich cover crops, and eliminate the need for using harmful, dangerous and expensive chemical fertilizers. They use crop rotation, allowing the soil to rest and replenish, to avoid pests and eliminate the need for dangerous and expensive pesticides.

The unnecessary chemicals from conventional agriculture, fertilizers and pesticides, negatively affect local wildlife, cause harmful runoff, pollute aquifers and waterways, and are harmful to human health. Financial incentives should be used instead to provide farmers with training in veganic /stock-free organic / natural agriculture. This should be a human and planetary health priority, and was never mentioned at the World Health Summit.

Political involvement and redirected subsidies can move the emphasis of food production away from unhealthy, pandemic inciting factory farming to small-scale natural plant farms owned and operated by the people previously marginalized by destructive animal agriculture. This would help encourage humans to eat healthful plant-based alternatives, reduce pollution, species extinction, habitat destruction, zoonotic disease, epidemics and pandemics, land degradation and desertification, and significantly reduce global warming.

Economists project implementing plant-based action programs would save significant sums of money. The University of Oxford calculates that eliminating animal-derived protein from the global food system would save $1.6 trillion in environmental costs by 2050. Most importantly, removing subsidies on innocent sentient individuals of other species exploited as food, would eliminate their unjust suffering, and redirect the Earth's unsustainable trajectory currently known as the Anthropocene Epoch.

5

Good Health For All Including The Planet

"Climate Change and Planetary Health", discussed at the Berlin World Health Summit, focused on the health of the environment. Scientific facts prove that methane traps heat in the atmosphere more effectively than carbon dioxide, making it the single greatest cause of global warming. Methane from animal agriculture, specifically the meat and dairy based diet is directly responsible for this impending disaster. The massive amount of animal feces produced in factory farms is the single greatest source of airborne methane, and global warming. It is unnecessary and preventable!

"The animal protein culture, conventionally viewed as improved consumption in a 'nutrition transition', has serious environmental and health consequences."
The Lancet

Animal agriculture is not only the main cause of global warming but it is also the single greatest factor in planetary destruction. It causes environmental degradation: desertification of land, destruction of forests, is responsible for pollution of air, water, and land, habitat destruction, species extinction, and biodiversity loss.

Loss of biodiversity is a factor in zoonotic disease. Species extinction from habitat destruction makes disease transmission between species more likely and more deadly. Zoonotic disease, the cause of epidemics and pandemics, is the result of disease transmission to humans from unjustly incarcerated and exploited animals.

Animal agriculture is destroying the planet. It is unsustainable, causes global warming and human disease, and requires extremely large amounts of land and water. Much less land and water is needed to grow plant-based food directly for human consumption. The underlying cause of the planet's problems result from humans' unjust treatment of nature, specifically, the most vulnerable individuals – those of other species.

The global livestock sector is growing faster than any other agriculture sub-sector, and with this and all other supremacist treatments of non-human species, comes disaster: climate change, planet degradation, and zoonotic pandemics. This does not take into consideration the immense suffering of the innocent individuals who are exploited to provide their unique individual bodies for human consumption, and other inhumane uses.

The key to assuring a healthy planet, and the health of individuals of all species on the planet, lies in restoring humanity's broken relationship with other species. This crucial fact was never mentioned at the Berlin World Health Summit.

6

Disaster of the Meat and Dairy Diet

Meat and dairy food production involves billions of high-risk interactions between humans and animals. Innocent, incarcerated animals in the food system are relentlessly stressed, confined, forced to share space with dead or diseased animals, share bodily fluids and airborne pathogens, expel waste on each other, all while being fed a steady supply of antibiotics. The physiological stress that animals endure weakens their immune systems, which makes them much more likely to become vectors of disease. The animal agriculture system invites zoonotic disaster!

According to the United Nations World Health Organization (WHO) the greatest threat to international health security is outbreaks of epidemic diseases. Factors fueling these outbreaks are the way food is produced and traded, and the way antibiotics are used and misused. There are an estimated 2 million drug-resistant infections that occur in the United States alone each year causing 23,000 human deaths.

These antibiotics originate from the literally billions of unjustly incarcerated and ultimately extrajudicially executed individuals raised as human food. Animal agriculture routinely puts antibiotics in their food and water to stimulate growth, while simultaneously enabling these unfortunate individuals to survive in the disease-ridden horrific conditions on factory farms.

Factory farms are epicenters of disease for humans as well as the billions of unfortunate animal individuals involuntarily incarcerated there. Thousands of genetically similar animals are packed together in unsanitary, overcrowded spaces. They are vulnerable to disease and stress placed on their immune systems by these horrific conditions.

Factory farms are ideal environments for viruses and other pathogens to circulate, mutate and 'spill over' to the human exploiters. United Nations Food and Agriculture Organization (FAO) maintains that farmed animals are the weakest link in our global food systems.

An estimated 99% of the ten billion land animals murdered for food every year are imprisoned in factory farms and murdered with impunity. Innocent animals in factory farms or live markets are severely stressed, cannot engage in natural behaviors, experience frustration, and maladaptive behaviors such as injuring or murdering one another out of survival instinct. Pigs can drop dead from the stress of being confined.

All these conditions make animals (amplifier hosts) more susceptible to pathogens, which then get passed on to their human abusers (bridge population), and then the human population in general through zoonotic pandemics.

Eating a meat and dairy based diet has been proven to cause the Non-Communicable Diseases (NCDs) of heart disease, diabetes, some cancers, obesity, and others. These avoidable morbidities are expensive to treat and now outnumber infectious diseases as the top killers globally. They cause nearly three-quarters of deaths in the world and kill approximately 41 million people every year.

Humans who eat a whole-foods, plant-based diet do not get the Non-Communicable Diseases (NCDs). Fat and cholesterol from eating other sentient beings fills the cells of humans making it impossible for those cells to accept nutritional glucose circulating in their blood to nourish all their cells, so it remains in their blood causing the symptoms of diabetes. This fat and cholesterol also fill the blood vessels causing the symptoms of heart disease. This overabundance of fat and cholesterol causes obesity.
Alternatively, a plant-based diet is rich in protein, fiber, vitamins, and minerals, has little fat, no cholesterol and looks and tastes delicious.

7

Global Health is a Political Issue

This vital idea was proposed by the World Health Summit, but the single most important political issue relating to global health - eliminating Speciesism - and moving beyond the Anthropocene Epoch by creating equity for all inhabitants on Earth, and including the planet itself, was never mentioned.

Epidemics, pandemics, Non-Communicable Diseases (NCDs), antibiotic resistance and other human health maladies, global issues of warming, pollution, desertification, biodiversity loss, habitat destruction and species extinction are all the direct result of speciesism – the abuse and exploitation of other species for the benefit of the human species.

The current human / animal relationship is unjust and unsustainable. This troubled relationship with animals keeps humanity at risk of zoonotic outbreaks, directly resulting from exploitation of animals and the environment we share with them.

What is needed is a comprehensive legal instrument that would address global health as a key political issue and would include human health, environmental and planetary health, as well as the health of all inhabitants on the planet, and the Earth itself. A United National Convention Against Speciesism and eventually an international law condemning speciesism would do this.

8 What Equity?

"Health Systems Resilience and Equity" was on the Berlin agenda, and the World Health Summit did an excellent job of dealing with the academic aspects of many issues, but there could have been more coverage on this important subject.

There is no 'equity' in the world when affluent people in the developed nations suffer from the costly and preventable diet related Non-Communicable Diseases (NCDs), and simultaneously non-affluent people in the developing nations suffer from the deadly, debilitating and inexpensive to treat Neglected Tropical Diseases (NTDs).

It is not uncommon for a single patient in a developed nation to incur hundreds of thousands of dollars-worth of health care for preventable heart disease and some cancers. Children and adults in the developing nations who suffer from the debilitating Tropical Diseases may need only a 50-cent pill once or twice a year. As a result of being unable to afford this medication, they become disabled for life. If this happens while they are children, they are deprived of an education and are totally dependent on others for the rest of their painful lives.

In addition, political subsidies in developed nations are notorious for causing poverty, hunger, and starvation in the developing nations. Worst of all, non-human sentient beings suffer from exploitation and lack of any rights. What equity?

9

Complex Dependency Between Climate, Food, Health and Justice

"Healthy Planet – Healthy People" is a transdisciplinary concept that addresses this issue as well as the impact of human disruptions to the Earth's natural systems on human health and all life on earth. It is an approach with aims to understand human impact on the world, how it can be addressed, and how the most urgent threat to global health – the triple crisis of climate change, pollution and biodiversity loss can be communicated and resolved.

The cause of human health crises: pandemics, Non-Communicable Diseases (which are currently responsible for most human mortality even compared to pandemics); planetary crises: global warming, pollution of air, water and land, habitat destruction, species extinction, and biodiversity loss, which are the major factors in zoonotic disease, and misuse of scarce resources, are all caused by Speciesism: abusing and exploiting other species for the benefit of the human species. Speciesism is destroying the planet and everyone on it, both humans and non-humans.

Hunger and starvation in developing nations could be avoided by using grain being fed to the unfortunate individuals raised to be 'food' in the developed nations, and instead feed that grain directly to the people who are exporting it at political subsidy induced artificially low prices while they and their children experience hunger, poverty, and starvation.

Exploiting animals is unjust and unsustainable. It requires more land, water and energy to raise animals for food than cultivating plant food for direct human consumption. One acre of land can yield between twelve and twenty times more plant food than animal-based foods.

"Global food production threatens climate stability and ecosystem resilience and constitutes the single largest driver of environmental degradation and transgression of planetary boundaries. A radical transformation of the global food system is urgently needed."

"The animal protein culture, conventionally viewed as improved consumption in a 'nutrition transition', has serious environmental and health consequences."

"Eating plants directly rather than in meat, dairy, eggs, much less of the crop is required to deliver the same amount of protein, without the pollution and pandemics."

The Lancet.

10 Lessons Learned

"Outsmarting Pandemics", as well as "Surveillance at the Animal – Human Interface", were presented at the Berlin World Health Summit, but they did not go far enough. They offered suggestions, but something as serious and life threatening as pandemics require more than mere suggestions.

Over the past 50 years, there has been a significant increase in the emergence of infectious diseases. More than 70% of emerging infectious diseases are zoonoses, diseases caused by germs that spread from exploited wild animals and farmed animals, to humans. Almost all of the pandemics known are zoonoses: SARS, MERS, Cov2, Ebola, Avian Flu, Swine Flu, Black Flu, and COVID-19, to name a few. These emergences and re-emergences are deeply linked to the pressures exerted on the environment, in particular on natural habitats and biodiversity. These pressures increase contacts between virus reservoirs in wildlife and livestock and humans.

No mention was made of the fact that all this is the result of Speciesism, the human exploitation of other species, destruction of their habitats, biodiversity loss caused by species extinction, and the only solution is to eliminate speciesism.

Speciesism is acting on the belief that humans are superior to all other species, and that humans can exercise complete control over every aspect of the non-humans. This prideful concept has brought humans and the planet to a precipice, which if not curtailed, would destroy both the humans, other species, nature, and the planet.

"The Cost of Inaction- The Importance of Pandemic Prevention at the Source" provided impressive statistics. Scientists calculate the costs of preventing further pandemics – via forest protection and improved wildlife trade regulation – over the next decade would amount to just 2% of the estimated financial damage caused by COVID 19.

Such prevention strategies would also come with considerable co-benefits for climate and biodiversity. Research shows the proportion of pathogens crossing from one stage to the next, from pre-emergence to pandemic stage decreases as the costs for stopping those increases. In this inverse correlation: the earlier we prevent the triple intersecting crises of health, climate, and biodiversity, the more cost efficient it will be.

This panel touched on important aspects of prevention but does not go far enough. An enforceable United Nations Convention Against Speciesism, and eventually an international law, would effectively prevent the next pandemic from happening, as well as promote biodiversity, reduce pollution, land degradation and reduce global warming and rising water levels.

"Strengthening Pandemic Preparedness and Response Lessons from Ebola and Covid-19

Outbreaks". This panel highlighted the importance of international collaboration in tackling global health threats but did not cover the single greatest means of prevention – avoidance. Zoonotic pandemics result from human – animal interactions. Exploiting and abusing animals is the cause of these pandemics. The best way to prepare for a pandemic is to avoid it by ending Speciesism.

"One Health in Action". The COVID-19 pandemic, the emergence of other zoonosis, along with increasing Antimicrobial Resistance (AMR) make it clear that an approach to the topic of health needs a broader understanding of the close links between the health of humans, animals, agriculture and the environment using the so called One Health approach. Since the diversity of species and habitats on Earth is vital to all life, including human life, it is essential to protect the natural environment in all its diversity, thereby lessening the risk of future pandemics and vector-borne diseases.

"The Role of Parliamentarians in the Development of A Global Pandemic Treaty" is an impressive idea. This Panel Discussion included Members of Parliament from Tanzania, United Arab Emirates, Cameroon, Argentina, and Germany. Although no definite steps were taken, an ongoing dialogue is very promising.

The most effective defense against pandemics is to eliminate their cause by the proposed United Nations Convention Against Speciesism advocated by Vegan International, as well as an international law similar to the Stop Ecocide law, currently being considered by the International Criminal Court.

11
Innovative Solutions to Health Challenges

"Stimulate Innovative Solutions to Health Challenges" was another issue covered by the Berlin World Health Summit. It was affirmed that recovery from COVID-19 presents a unique opportunity for transformative change. Initiatives and advances in non-Anthropocene Earth-Centered Law which could fill this void by protecting the rights of all species, thus preventing pandemics, and changing the destructive trajectory the Earth is currently on, were not discussed.

International Laws to protect the rights of all species are innovative solutions to the health challenges presented by species exploitation which include zoonotic pandemics, the Non-Communicable Diseases (NCDs), other illnesses, as well as global warming caused by methane, pollution of air, water and land, species extinction, biodiversity loss, and habitat destruction. Contemporary thinking, including that at the World Health Summit, has not reached this conclusion yet.

Giving all inhabitants on planet Earth, as well as the Earth itself, enforceable rights is the only innovative solution which makes any sense. Health challenges have many causes, most of which could be resolved by moving past the Anthropocene Epoch.

Unfortunate non-human individuals are unjustly incarcerated in disease ridden, horrific conditions, subjected to mutilation, violation, rape, kidnap of their children, and ultimately horrifically murdered, usually while fully conscious, all to satisfy the whims of those in power – the humans, who are making themselves and the planet increasingly unhealthy in the process. Their lives are calling out for justice, and we are experiencing a portion of that justice now in the global health issues we are facing. The human species will not experience peace or safety while continuing to exploit other species.

This heedless dominion over the Earth is simply not sustainable. Feeding much of the world's edible grain crop to unjustly incarcerated farmed individuals while vulnerable humans starve or are malnourished is not only inexcusable injustice but is a grossly inefficient and unsustainable use of natural resources, simultaneously creating mounting human health, pollution, and global warming problems.

Everyone deserves justice, and a United Nations 'Place at the Table', regardless of species. 'No One Left Behind', should apply to everyone on planet Earth, not just to one species. There needs to be a radical, comprehensive approach to sustaining human health and preventing destruction of the planet.

A shift to the plant-based diet, and giving animals universal rights, would promote sustainability, and remove the specter of pandemic zoonotic disease. Animals, birds and fish, humans' co-habitants on Earth, are

the least protected, most exploited
individuals on a planet that is currently
headed for disaster if radical changes are not
implemented.

12 What Peace?

"Global Health For Peace" was on the agenda at the World Health Summit. This is an often over looked topic. and its importance is not sufficiently emphasized.

According to United Nations Secretary General Antonio Guterres:

 "Non-human animals are sentient beings not mere property and must be afforded respect and legal recognition."

"Making peace with nature is the defining task of the 21st century."

This aspect of global peace is woefully neglected, and dismissed in most discussions on Peace, including at the World Health Summit. There can be no peace while there is an ongoing war on the non-human species. Exerting human superiority over nature and other species, is a form of war. It is only when human pride is surpassed by compassion, if necessary, by enforceable laws, that global health and peace for all will ever occur.

Global peace and health initiatives will be useless unless they include a peaceful, virtuous and harmonious coexistence between humans, nature, and all other sentient beings on the planet. Peace must be extended to all species and also to nature in general. This was conspicuously absent from World Health Summit discussions.

Everyone deserves justice, and a United Nations' 'Place at the Table', regardless of species. The United Nations motto, 'No One Left Behind', should apply to everyone on planet Earth, not just to one species. There needs to be a radical, comprehensive approach to promoting Peace for all on planet Earth.

Exploited animals are innocent individuals who suffer the loss of their children, rape and violation of their bodies, experience fear and pain, are tortured and murdered with impunity, and have absolutely no recourse. These unfortunate individuals are unjustly incarcerated in disease ridden, horrific conditions, subjected to mutilation, kidnap of their children, and ultimately murdered

horrifically, usually while fully conscious,
all to satisfy the whims of those in power –
the humans who are making themselves and
the planet increasingly unhealthy in the
process.

Exploitation of innocent individuals of other
species is an unjust war on the defenseless.
This war is a global health, peace, and a
justice issue. They are calling out for
justice, and we are experiencing a portion of
that justice now in the serious global health
issues we are currently facing.

Speciesism, war on other species, is
unhealthy, unjust, unsustainable, and
destructive. It is treating animals as slaves
of humans. The unfortunate individuals,
who are eaten, used for clothing,
experiments, and entertainment, have no
rights of their own, and deserve to have such
rights. They have complex social and
psychological lives, have families, and feel
pain just as humans do. They are victims of
exploitation, murder, species extinction, and
habitat destruction. Animals are the least
protected and most exploited individuals on

the planet – a planet that is currently on a trajectory headed for disaster if radical changes are not implemented. These individuals are our co-inhabitants on planet Earth. They deserve rights, the United Nations 'Place at the Table', and not to be 'Left Behind'.

The United Nations Sustainable Development Goal 16 (SDG 16) 'Peace and Justice' currently does not include all individuals on Earth. Peace is only applied to the human species. This is not only an outrageous injustice, but also threatens the very existence of human life through zoonotic pandemics linked to unjust treatment of other species and spilling over to the human species, as well as destroying planet Earth through methane induced climate change, destruction of land, and pollution of air, water, and land. Global Health and Peace will not happen until there is peace with all individuals of all species on Earth, and all individuals of all species have rights, and everyone of all species is finally given a 'Place at the Table'.

13

Summit Food Service
Exemplified Optimal Health

"Food Systems and Health" was rightly recognized by The Berlin World Health Summit. It was affirmed that food choices affect the health of everyone, including the planet. The Summit inadvertently provided the most practical and delicious examples of sustainable, healthful food in the buffets, snacks and lunches served by the Hotel Central District Berlin which hosted the Summit. The Hotel provided extremely attractive, delicious buffets, snacks and gourmet lunches consisting of fruit and vegetables artfully prepared and decorated, and purchased from sustainable local farms and businesses.

Even the tables were attractively decorated with fresh fruit, vegetables, and terra cotta pots of pungent herbs. No one complained that there was no meat and extremely little dairy in the food served. In fact, these fabulous, imaginative works of art disappeared quickly into the welcoming hands and mouths of the Conference participants.

None of these plant-based offerings were ever boring or unappetizing, including the lowly potatoes, elevated to new heights. Everything was gorgeous, imaginative, delicious, elegant and imaginatively named. Even the center pieces were inspirations – artistically arranged cauliflower heads, fresh tomatoes, and squash from sustainable sourced local farms and businesses, as well as terra cotta pots of fresh herbs, which decorated the tables and buffets.

The buffets at the World Health Summit taught the most practical lesson of all the high-level meetings. The simple answer to the complex problems of health and environmental issues is the delicious, attractive and healthful Plant-Based Lifestyle

14

Cognitive Dissonance at

Sharm El-Sheikh

It is an undisputed fact documented by the United Nations Food and Agriculture Organization (UN FAO) that animal agriculture is the leading cause of Climate Change. This undisputable fact was not only absent from the discussions at the 2022 Congress of the Parties (COP 27) Climate Change Conference, but according to a COP 27 attendee, the most serious contributor to climate change – beef - was served extensively to Conference attendees.

The United Nations Food and Agriculture Organization Report, Livestock's Long Shadow, which is more than 300 pages, documents the impacts of the world's livestock on the environment, and the very significant contribution of animal agriculture to climate change, pollution of air, land, and soil, livestock induced deforestation and desertification, water degradation, and biodiversity loss.

According to this FAO report published in 2006, the livestock sector emerges as one of the most significant contributors to serious environmental problems on every scale from local to global including climate change. Livestock's contribution to environmental problems is on a massive scale and "needs to be addressed with urgency". The livestock sector is responsible for 18% of greenhouse gas emissions measured in CO_2 equivalent, which is a higher share than transportation. Livestock are responsible for much larger shares of some gasses with far higher potential to warm the atmosphere, and it is growing significantly.

The livestock sector is by far the single largest anthropogenic user of land, and is a key player in increased water use. It is the largest sectoral source of water pollution, contributing to 'dead zones' in coastal areas. Major sources of pollution are from animal waste, antibiotics and hormones, chemicals from tanneries, fertilizers and pesticides used for feed crops, and sediments from eroded pastures. The report suggests animal agriculture should be a major policy issue when dealing with problems of climate change, pollution, misuse of scarce resources, and loss of biodiversity.

Rising demand for food products of animal origins caused by growing incomes along with changing food preferences are increasing demand for meat and dairy livestock products and increasing the level of damage and adverse impact on the environment. According to FAO, "Livestock products are a contributing cause of obesity." The meat and dairy based diet is also linked to the Non Communicable Diseases (NCDs) of diabetes, heart disease, and some cancers, as well as being the single greatest cause of global warming. Eating animals is unhealthy for humans, the planet, and most definitely for the innocent animals.

The World Health Organization said the pivotal climate talks at COP 27 issues a grim reminder that the climate crisis continues to make people sick, jeopardizes human lives, and that human health must be at the core of these critical negotiations, Climate change is already affecting people's health and will continue to do so at an accelerating rate unless urgent action is taken. The most effective urgent action to take is to ban animal agriculture and to encourage humans to adopt a plant-based diet.

"Climate change is making millions of people sick or more vulnerable to disease all over the world and the increasing destructiveness of extreme weather events disproportionately affects poor and marginalized communities," said Dr Tedros Adhanom Ghebreyesus, WHO Director-General.

Small Island Nations are the most effected by global warming and suffering the most. To their credit, they are fighting back. Vanuatu has started an initiative to Stop Ecocide by making it a crime punishable by the International Criminal Court. The Minister of Health from Fiji is quoted as saying once culture is lost, it is gone forever. Vegan International hopes that these and other nations will see the connection between animal agriculture, ecocide, and global warming, and also make that speciesism an international crime.

If energy is the problem, Sustainable Energy For All (SE4All) has the solutions! Their SDG 7 Pavilion at the COP 27 Conference offered an opportunity to engage and discuss topics of importance to a just and equitable energy transition. They showcased how to unite global efforts on energy, climate, and development. The SE4All initiatives were aimed at ending energy poverty and supporting climate progress by reducing the contribution of energy to global warming.

This admirable common sense and innovative thinking should be used on the real global warming problem: animal agriculture.

15
SAGO: The Best
The World Has To Offer

The Scientific Advisory Group for the
Origins of Novel Pathogens (SAGO) was
established in 2021 to 'provide technical and
scientific considerations regarding emerging
and re-emerging pathogens and, in this
capacity, to advise the World Health
Organization (WHO) on prioritizing studies
and field investigations into the origins of
such pathogens, as per their terms of
reference.'

The Scientific Advisory Group for the
Origins of novel pathogens (SAGO)
provided recommendations on studies that
need to be conducted in order to better
understand the origins of zoonotic viruses.
None of these studies focused on their
Anthropocene origins: human supremacy
over nonhuman individuals.

The key recommendations of the SAGO
reports focused on conducting clinical and

epidemiological retrospective studies to better define the role of human-to-human transmission dynamics and drivers for zoonotic disease spread, and explore its potential spread to the first cases discovered in newly affected countries. They reviewed clinical and laboratory records, set targets in locations where cases were detected, and searched for early cases that could have been missed.

SAGO reviewed samples from historical cases, used metadata links to clinical histories, and performed phylogenetic studies to understand viral mutation patterns and the emergence of additional viruses with changes, and the effect of co-infections.

Additionally, SAGO conducted infectiousness studies to identify the reproductive number, duration of viral shedding and all possible transmission routes. They conducted multidisciplinary and multisectoral zoonosis studies to identify animal reservoirs and animal sources of infection in endemic and non-endemic regions to understand the role of animal-to-human transmission.

SAGO conducted environmental, anthropological (the study of humankind; human caused), behavioral and social science studies around confirmed cases to better understand how zoonotic disease is transmitted between humans.

Not once did SAGO focus on the obvious – zoonotic disease is caused by human exploitation of non-humans, and the solution is to stop exploiting other species by granting them enforceable rights. Is this the best scientific research that the world has to offer? It completely missed the obvious. However, they did work hard, cover lot of bases, and no doubt expended an exorbitant amount of money.

16

Biodiversity and
Ecosystem Health

In May 2019, the Intergovernmental
Science-Policy Platform on Biodiversity and
Ecosystem Services (IPBES), the
intergovernmental body which assesses the
state of Nature, released the first-ever
intergovernmental global assessment on the
health of biodiversity and ecosystems.

In its report documenting Nature's
dangerous decline, the Platform emphasized
that the disappearance of pollinator species
and freshwater fish, and the eradication of
forest ecosystems would drastically affect
human life, threaten the food supply,
exacerbate global warming and disease
transmission, in many ways which are not
yet fully understood. It highlighted that the
unprecedented species extinction rates are
accelerating. Currently 1,000,000 species

are threatened with extinction according to Reuters World News Today.

The report contained a call for fundamental, system-wide reorganization across technological, economic and social factors, including re-evaluating paradigms, goals and values. The ISPPBES emphasized that current global responses are insufficient, and that transformative changes are needed to restore and protect nature. Fierce opposition from vested interests needs to be overcome for the public good. As we know, this is easier said than done!

Nonetheless, social and cultural value changes are fundamental to the future of humankind and to how humans navigate both climate change and future pandemics. The key to sustainability and to assuring a healthy planet, lies in restoring humanity's broken relationship with the land and with Nature as a whole, and in particular with other species.

Humans must be willing to reevaluate their consumption, give other species enforceable rights, and be willing to stop considering Nature as an object for manipulation and exploitation, in order to truly protect biodiversity, ecosystems, and prevent the destruction of the entire planet and all those on the planet.

17

Livestock's Long Shadow

Livestock's Long Shadow Environmental Issues and Options is a more than 300-page report compiled by the Food and Agriculture Organization of the United Nations (UN FAO), dated 29 November 2006, in Rome, Italy. The premise is that livestock is a major threat to the environment, and that remedies are urgently needed.

According to Livestock's Long Shadow, the livestock sector generates more greenhouse gas emissions than all of transportation. Livestock is also shown to be a major source of land and water degradation.

According to Henning Steinfeld, Chief of FAO's Livestock Information and Policy Branch and Senior Author of the report: "Livestock are one of the most significant contributors to today's most serious environmental problems. Urgent action is required to remedy the situation."

With increased prosperity, people are consuming more meat and dairy products every year. Global meat production is projected to more than double from 229 million tons in 1999/2001 to 465 million tons in 2050, while milk output is set to climb from 580 to 1043 million tons according to David Robinson Simon in "Meatonomics".

The global livestock sector is growing faster than any other agriculture sub-sector. Such rapid growth exacts a steep environmental price, according to the FAO report, Livestock's Long Shadow – Environmental Issues and Options. "The Environmental costs per unit of livestock production must be cut by one half, just to avoid the level of damage worsening beyond its present level".

When emissions from land use and land use change are included, the livestock sector accounts for 9 percent of CO_2 deriving from human-related activities but produces a much larger share of even more harmful greenhouse gases. It generates 65 percent of human-related nitrous oxide, which has 296 times the Global Warming Potential of CO_2. Most of this comes from animal feces.

According to FAO, raising livestock, so called animal agriculture, accounts for approximately 37 percent of all human induced methane which is at least 23 times as warming as CO_2, and is largely produced by the digestive system and urine of these individuals. The ammonia from this urine contributes significantly to acid rain.

Livestock now use 30 percent of the earth's entire land surface which is mostly permanent pasture. Additionally it also uses 33 percent of the global arable land to produce crops to feed livestock, the report notes. Forests are cleared to create new pastures, which is the major driver of deforestation. In Latin America, for example, 70 percent of the former forests in the Amazon have been turned over to grazing. Previously the Amazon was considered a reliable source of global cooling. That is now gone to provide steak for affluent humans (ie. warm affluent humans).

Herds of sentient individuals raised to be murdered and consumed by Anthropocene individuals, cause wide-scale land degradation. Currently about 20 percent of pastures are considered degraded and useless due to overgrazing, and are compacted, and eroded. This figure is even higher in drylands where inappropriate policies and inadequate livestock management contributed to advanced desertification. Land degradation is almost always irreversible.

The livestock business is among the most damaging sectors to the earth's increasingly scarce water resources, contributing among other things to water pollution, and euthropication - excessive richness of nutrients in a lake or other body of water, frequently due to runoff from the land causing a dense growth of plant life and death of animal life from lack of oxygen. and the degeneration of coral reefs. The major polluting agents are animal urine, feces, blood, antibiotics and hormones, chemicals from tanneries, fertilizers and pesticides used in feed crop production. Widespread overgrazing disturbs water cycles, and reduces replenishment of above and below ground water resources. Additionally, significantly larger amounts of the scarce resource of water are used in the production of livestock for food than in the more sustainable plant-based agriculture.

Livestock are estimated to be the main inland source of phosphorous and nitrogen contamination of oceans and waterways, significantly contributing to biodiversity loss in marine ecosystems.

Sentient animals raised for meat and dairy now account for about 20 percent of all terrestrial animal biomass. Livestock's presence in vast tracts of land, and their need for feed crops, is a major contributor to biodiversity loss. Many important ecosystem services are considered in decline, with animals involunatraily raised to be eaten by humans identified as the main cause.

This FAO report does not take into consideration the immense suffering of these innocent individuals who are exploited to provide their bodies for human consumption. This 'diet' then causes human heart disease, diabetes, some cancers, as well as obesity, antibiotic resistance and often depression in those humans who choose to eat these innocent exploited individuals. Habitat loss to provide room for these unfortunates is a major contributor to biodiversity loss and species extinction, as well as global warming from eliminating the cooling effect of forests.

18

Zoonotic Disease is
Human Initiated

Zoonotic diseases, including Covid-19, SARS, MERS, Ebola, Human Immunodeficiency Virus (HIV), Acquired Immunodeficiency Syndrome (AIDS), Avian Flu, Swine Flu, Black Flu, Spanish Flu, are the direct result of the unjust systematic abuse and exploitation of other species by the human species.

Zoonotic diseases, the cause of most epidemics and pandemics, are caused by human – animal interaction. Globally, many of the most serious infectious diseases are zoonotic, causing an estimated 3 million human deaths per year before the current Covid-19 pandemic. A zoonotic disease is caused by a pathogen that jumps, or "spills over", from animals to humans. Infections are then transmitted directly among humans.

Pathogens include prions, viruses, bacteria, protozoa, parasites, and fungi. Zoonotic disease may be vector born, foodborne, or waterborne.

Emerging diseases are almost invariably zoonotic. An estimated 60% of all viruses that infect humans came from animals, and 75% of all new infectious diseases in the past decade are zoonotic. Examples include Covid-19, Human Immunodeficiency Virus (HIV), Ebola virus, SARS, MERS, Swine Flu, and Avian Flu, among many, many others. Zoonoses have caused the deadliest pandemics in history: Black Death, Spanish Flu, HIV, and now Covid-19. The global rate of zoonotic disease is increasing. Without understanding the creation and spread of zoonoses, and rectifying these issues, it is impossible to prevent the next pandemic.

COVID-19 originated from an animal in a live animal market. Scientific evidence indicates that the virus originated from a bat coronavirus, then transferred to an intermediate host, either a wild or domestic animal, either in the wild, or kept in captivity. It ultimately evolved into SARS-CoV-2, the coronavirus responsible for COVID-19, and spread to humans.

HIV/AIDS, also from zoonotic origins, is one of the most serious public health threats. More than 33 million people worldwide are infected with HIV and more than 25 million people have died from the disease. HIV/AIDS originated when an established SIV switched from primates to humans through exposure to blood or other secretions of infected primates. This occurred through the hunting and butchering of innocent wild animals. Bites and other injuries caused by primates kept as pet animals can cause a viral transmission according to 'Future Medicine'.

Ebola virus disease (EVD), also from zoonotic origins, is a deadly disease with outbreaks that occur primarily on the African continent. It is caused by an infection with a group of viruses within the genus *Ebolavirus*: according to the Center for Disease Control and Prevention (CDC).

Bird / Avian Flu (H5N1) in 1997, and Swine Flu (H1N1) in 2009 emerged from agricultural facilities - factory farms - with horrific conditions. H5N1 has an estimated mortality rate of 60 percent, and could easily mutate and become more lethal. H1N1 is believed to have originated in pigs in North Carolina resulting in more than 200,000 infections and 18,000 human deaths, including 250 children. The innocent, exploited pigs and birds suffered much higher casualties! According to the World Health Organization (Who), the 1997 outbreak of H5N1 resulted in the death of an estimated 1.5 million chickens and other birds. The infamous 'Great Influenza' of 1918 – 1919, also zoonotic, sickened one-third of the world's population and resulted in the death of over 50 million people. The horrific exploitation, suffering and deaths of countless domestic and wild birds was the cause.

Modern food production involves billions of high-risk interactions between humans and animals. Innocent, incarcerated animals in the food system are relentlessly stressed, confined, forced to share space with dead or diseased animals, share bodily fluids and airborne pathogens, expel waste on each other, all while being fed a steady supply of antibiotics. The physiological stress that animals endure weakens their immune systems making them much more likely to become vectors of disease. The system invites zoonotic disaster.

Factory farms are epicenters of disease for humans as well as the billions of unfortunate animals involuntarily incarcerated there. Thousands of genetically similar animals are packed together in unsanitary, overcrowded spaces. They are vulnerable to disease and stress placed on their immune systems by these horrific conditions. Factory farms are ideal environments for viruses and other pathogens to circulate, mutate and 'spill over' to human exploiters. United Nations Food and Agriculture Organization (FAO) maintains that farmed animals are the weakest link in our global health.

An estimated 99% of the ten billion land animals murdered for food every year in the US alone are imprisoned in factory farms, and murdered with impunity. Innocent animals in factory farms or live markets are severely stressed, cannot engage in natural behaviors, experience frustration, and maladaptive behaviors such as injuring or murdering one another out of survival instinct. Pigs can drop dead from the stress of being confined. All these conditions make animals (amplifier hosts) more susceptible to pathogens, which then get passed on to their human abusers (bridge population), and the human population in general through pandemics.

Live Markets, or 'wet markets', offer the sale and on-site slaughter of a multitude of innocent animals, including rare and wild animals. This often includes endangered or threatened wild animals, and other animals who would never come into contact with one another in the wild. These markets exist all over the world. Covid-19 is believed to have started in one in Wuhan, China. Customers purchase and murder innocent animals for both human consumption and traditional Chinese medicine.

Eighty percent of the antibiotics produced worldwide are fed to unjustly incarcerated animals raised to be consumed by humans. As a result, people suffer antibiotic resistant infections, with a high percentage resulting in mortality. This is in addition to the unparalleled suffering being caused to the sentient beings forced to endure this insanity. It is now well established that abuse of antibiotics fosters new antibiotic resistant diseases for which people will eventually have no defense. According to the World Health Organization (WHO) 'We are headed for a post-antibiotic era, in which common infections and minor injuries can once again kill.'

The widespread routine use of manure as fertilizer, and irrigation with contaminated water is a real concern. Salmonella and E. coli can spread to vegetables and contaminate them. Veganic agriculture uses no animal inputs. Instead, it uses 'green manure' - plowed under nitrogen rich cover crops. Pathogen runoff from intense animal imprisonment can permeate human water supplies leading to bacterial contamination of rivers and streams impacting both humans and wildlife. These pathogens include fecal coliforms, Streptococcus, Campylobacter, Giardia, Cryptosporidium, E. coli, as well as viruses, all resulting from the unjust exploitation of other species.

Zoonotic pandemics are inevitable, given the increasing incursion of human beings into wildlife habitat. 75% of earth's land areas have already been heavily transformed by human activity. Species are presently going extinct at approximately 1,000 times the natural rate. Habitat destruction, biodiversity loss, and humanity's attendant encroachment on wildlands adds to the risk of zoonotic disease. Scientists agree that habitat loss is positively correlated with increased zoonotic disease. This is because high biodiversity reduces the risk of zoonotic disease by the 'Dilution Effect'. High biodiversity actually protects human health by reducing the risk of zoonotic disease.

The current human / animal relationship is unjust and unsustainable. This troubled relationship with animals keeps humanity at risk of zoonotic outbreaks, directly resulting from exploitation of animals and the environment we share with them. There is no way to humanely and safely confine and exploit animals. This has not worked. The United Nations recommendation of stricter regulations of live markets, the UN Universal Declaration of Animal Welfare, and global investigations have not been effective in solving the problem. What is needed is a radical, comprehensive approach.

The human species will not experience peace or real safety while continuing to exploit and degrade other species. Everyone deserves justice, and 'a place at the table' regardless of species. 'No one left behind' should apply to everyone on planet Earth, not just to one species. There needs to be a radical, comprehensive approach: a United Nations Convention Against Speciesism

Stephen S. Morse et al, Zoonoses, The Lancet; Zoonotic Diseases, CDC; WHO/FAO/OIE Report of the Joint Consultation on Emerging Zoonotic Diseases; Aysha Akhtar, Animals and Public Health Why Treating Animals Better is Critical To Human Welfare; Center of the Deadly Coronavirus Outbreak, Time Magazine; WHO, H5N1 Avian Influenza: Time-line of major events.

19

Starvation of Vulnerable Linked To Diet of Affluent

Of planet Earth's nearly 8 billion humans, roughly 1 billion people are malnourished, and 6 million children starve to death annually as a result of the meat and dairy based diet of the affluent.

Farming sentient animal individuals is notoriously wasteful when compared to growing plants to feed humans directly. Livestock animals - individuals raised for meat and dairy - take drastically more food from the global food supply than they provide. Crops necessary to feed individuals raised for human food are vastly more crops than it would take to feed humans directly. It takes thirteen pounds of grain to yield just one pound of beef. Crops such as soy and lentils produce as much protein as beef, and often more, without the waste of water and land, and pollution of air, water and land.

Feeding half the world's edible grain crop to unjustly incarcerated farmed individuals is grossly inefficient, and a waste of natural resources. It requires far more land, water and energy than cultivating plant food for direct human consumption. One acre of land can yield between twelve and twenty times more plant food than animal-based foods. This is also true of water usages. Pollution of water, air and land, human mortality and morbidity, as well as starvation of the world's most vulnerable people also result from the affluents' meat and dairy based diet.

The equation is simple: crops can be fed to people or animals, but not both. Crops that are fed to animals to feed affluent individuals could be fed to poor, hungry, or starving adults and children, but not both.

Part Two

The Cause - Supremacy

20

Language and Supremacy

What can you learn from language? Is it the underpinning of mindset, philosophy, and human behavior. The way individuals act, the things they do, the choices they make, are all a linked to their language. Humans think in their language. It is that thinking which governs their choices and actions. Language shapes the relationship between humans, non-humans, the environment, and the entire planet.

Specifically, 30% of English and Romance languages are verbs and 70% are nouns, while 70% of Indigenous languages are verbs and 30% are nouns. Many Romance languages further divide nouns into male and female gender. Speaking English or Romance languages gives the speaker implicit permission to disregard and disrespect other species, and nature in general. The language itself is supremacist.

It only follows logically that speakers of these languages will have an innate tendency to supremacy.

The grammar of animacy is not found in English or Romance languages which reduce words to either human or thing. Indigenous languages divide languages into animate and inanimate, with animate being everything natural, humans, animals, plants, fire, rocks, winds, and more. This gives them a greater respect for nature, and this respect and reverence leads to a closer bond with nature, and a willingness not to abuse, disrespect, overharvest, or overuse natural resources.

Indigenous languages are verb centered. Verbs imply life, movement, and choices. Noun centered languages foster a culture of supremacy: I, we, she, he, etc. are the most important.

Robin Wall Kimmerer is an American Distinguished Teaching Professor of Environmental and Forest Biology, and the Director of the Center for Native Peoples and the Environment at the State University of New York College of Environmental Science and Forestry (SUNY-ESF). Kimmerer is the author of numerous scientific articles, and the books: "Gathering Moss: A Natural and Cultural History of Mosses", "Braiding Sweetgrass: Indigenous Wisdom", and "Scientific Knowledge and the Teachings of Plants". She is citizen and an enrolled member of the Potawatomi Nation. Ms. Kimmerer combines her heritage with her scientific and environmental passions.

In her book, "Braiding Sweet Grass", Author Robin Wall Kimmerer shares her belief that indigenous teaching can inform modern science and community building, particularly when it comes to efforts to preserve the natural world and fight climate change. Ms. Kimmerer also explores the tension between traditional indigenous conceptions of biology and the modern, scientific modes of addressing this subject.

Language and small ceremonies were used by indigenous people in order to conceive of the world in a different manner. The indigenous interpretation emphasizes the symbiosis between the natural world and humanity known as 'reciprocity'.

By recognizing and appreciating reciprocity in nature, humans may eventually replicate these patterns in their social and economic structures. Robin Wall Kimmerer believes that market economies based around private property should be replaced with the "gift economies" evident in many modern and ancestral indigenous communities. She believes that through giving and receiving gifts, as opposed to buying and selling commodities, humanity may learn to appreciate the preciousness of the Earth's bounty, and to practice restraint in extracting resources, and thus stave off the ruinous consequences of overconsumption.

Language is both an important motif and valuable tool for living in greater harmony with Nature. It promotes a paradigm shift suggesting that humanity alter the way it conceives of the world in order to save it.

Native science holds that leadership is rooted not in power and authority but in service and wisdom She hopes that indigenous culture can supplement non-indigenous norms for the purpose of creating a more harmonious and reciprocal relationship between humanity and nature.

Anton Treuer is a descendant of the Leech Lake Band of Ojibwe tribe, whose lands border the small city of Bemidji, Minnesota, in the heart of the Deep North. Just as the Deep South is associated with racial antipathy, so too is the great expanse of land spanning Northern Michigan, Wisconsin and Minnesota for native Americans. Surrounded by three Ojibwe reservations – Leech Lake, Red Lake and White Earth – Bemidji is a border town predominantly white and well known for racial hostility towards native people.

Despite Treuer's good grades and test scores, his white high school counsellors advocated vocational training not college. He applied to, and was accepted by,

Princeton University! He put his acceptance letter on the wall outside his counsellor's office. After Treuer graduated from Princeton University, he earned a Doctorate in history from the University of Minnesota.

Anton Treuer is currently a Professor of Ojibwe (a Native American Language) at Bemidji State University in Minnesota. He is the Author of "The Language Warrior's Manifesto", and fourteen other books on Indigenous history, language, and culture including: "Living Our Language: Ojibwe Tales and Oral Histories", "Everything You Wanted to Know about Indians but Were Afraid to Ask", "The Assassination of Hole in the Day", and "Oshkaabewis Native Journal".

According to Treuer, "Language and culture go hand in hand. There is no way to separate a language from its culture…ways of thinking…and material goods. Languages embody unique worldviews…and is the key to everything in culture."

"Everyone needs to heal and interrupt the colonial process, which dehumanizes us all. White folks need healing. They are the primary beneficiaries of the systems of oppression operating in the world today. It hurts more to be a victim of oppression than a beneficiary, but oppression dehumanizes everyone. Language can disrupt the glue for colonial thinking which has been fundamentally dehumanizing to indigenous people", he explains.

"Instead of fighting over the transfer of power from one group to another, we should seek to transform the nature of power entirely. Instead of squabbling over who will be the oppressor, we should all be working collectively to fight oppression", he said.

These words of wisdom from indigenous thinkers could benefit everyone involved in the unsustainable trajectory this planet is currently on. Unhealthy use of power not only applies to human relations but also relations with other species and with nature in general.

21

The Banality of Supremacy

Supremacy, the major cause of most of the Anthropocene Earth's ills, stems from pride - a misguided belief of self-importance and entitlement, often coupled with the power to enforce that belief on others. This includes beliefs that one sex is stronger or more competent that the other, that one race is better, more beautiful, or more important than others, that one nationality is more deserving of earthly goods at the expense of others having less, or the destructive belief that one species deserves everything while other species are entitled to nothing. This human evil - pride - has caused wars, genocides, exploitation of individuals, races, nations and species. Without reining in the evil of human supremacy, planet Earth will never move beyond the Anthropocene Epoch.

History is full of evidence of the human evil, supremacy, these are only a few:

On August 6, 1945, and on August 9, 1945, respectively United States B-29 bombers, dropped the world's first and second atomic bombs over the Japanese cities of Hiroshima and Nagasaki. The explosions immediately killed an estimated 80,000 innocent people, and tens of thousands more died later due to radiation. At that point, the war was effectively over. Japan was no longer a military threat to the United States.

No nuclear bombs were dropped in Europe where the physical features of those humans were similar to the United States humans who dropped the bombs. Additionally, Japanese-Americans were incarcerated in internment camps during World War II, unlike their German-American counterparts. Conditions in these camps were so severe that one in four infants born there perished.

March 16, 1968. The My Lai massacre was the mass murder of more than 500 unarmed Vietnamese civilians by United States troops. Victims included men, women, children, and infants. Some of the women were gang-raped and their bodies mutilated. Some mutilated and raped children were as young as 12. Again, the facial features were different.

In 1974 the Hutu majority in Rwanda murdered from 500,000 to 1 million innocent civilian Tutsis and moderate Hutus, and caused the migration of two million Hutus. It started in Kigali, the capital, and spread throughout the country. Ordinary citizens were incited by local officials to take up arms against their ethnically 'inferior' neighbors.

In 1915, during World War I, 'ethnically different' Armenians were systematically killed or deported by the Turks of the Ottoman Empire.

Between 1976 and 1983 in Argentina, children 'disappeared'. Many babies were kidnapped with their parents or after their parents were killed. Others were born in clandestine detention centers where their mothers were taken. These disappeared children, born into a 'lower class', were deprived of their identity, religion, right to live with their family, and all of the rights that are nationally and internationally recognized as universal human rights. They were, however, often adopted by childless couples from the prevailing 'upper class'. This evil finally ended due to relentless efforts by the children's grandmothers.

From 1975 to 1979 in Cambodia, almost two million political prisoners suspected of connections with the former government or foreign governments were executed or died from disease and starvation. They were buried by the Khmer Rouge regime in the so-called Killing Fields at the end of the Cambodian Civil War.

The Holocaust of World War II in Europe was Nazi Germany's deliberate, organized, state-sponsored persecution and machinelike murder of approximately six million European Jews and at least five million Soviet Prisoners of War, Catholics, Romany, Jehovah's Witnesses, Gays, and other victims who were culturally, religiously or politically 'inferior' and 'undesirable'.

Between 1920 and 1953 in the Soviet Union, approximately 4.2 million people were victims of political purges. Two million were killed or imprisoned in 1937 and 1938 alone when Josef Stalin's campaign of terror against 'undesirables' was at its height.

These are only a few examples of history's evidence of destructive supremacist evil.

The number of human individuals victimized by supremacist evil is in the millions.

The number of non-human individuals victimized by human supremacy is in the

Billions

... per year... per developed nation!

These unjustly victimized non-human sentient beings had mothers, children, families and were unjustly deprived of their lives. They have been systematically subjected to bestiality, rape, kidnap, incarceration, torture, murder, all with impunity, simply because they did not belong to the supremacist human species. Their bodies have been eaten, used as milk machines, and laboratory equipment. They have been bred to be many times their normal size, forced to menstruate hundreds of times more than normal. Their skin has been used as coats, shoes and bags. In the process, this abnormal manipulation of nature has contributed to global warming and pollution, and misuse of scarce resources.

Now the questions: Is it an act 'evil' if it is done by a 'good' person? Or, can a 'good' person do 'evil' deeds?

'The Banality of Evil' by Hannah Arendt puts forward the question 'Can anyone do evil without being evil?' Arendt addressed this question in 1961 when she reported on the war crimes trial of Adolph Eichmann, for *The New Yorker*.

Otto Adolf Eichmann was an Schutzstaffel (SS) Obersturmbannfuhrer (which corresponds to Lieutenant Colonel) and the Nazi responsible for organizing the transportation of millions of Jews, Catholics, Gypsies, Gays, and those heroic individuals who fought to oppose the Nazis, to concentration camps where they were systematically incarcerated, tortured and murdered with impunity.

Arendt found Eichmann an ordinary, rather bland, bureaucrat, who in her words, was 'neither perverted nor sadistic', but 'terrifyingly normal', and she felt his only motive was to advance his career in the Nazi bureaucracy. Others disputed this, including Raoul Wallenberg, the World War II Hero responsible for saving 100,000 innocent lives during the last six months in 1945. Wallenberg had first-hand knowledge of Eichmann and his evil deeds.

Arednt believed Eichmann performed these evil deeds without evil intentions, just 'thoughtlessness', or disengagement from the reality of his evil acts. Therefore, it follows that seemingly 'normal' people can act in extremely evil ways.

Ordinary people can be capable of great evil. All humans have the capacity to embrace or avoid evil. It is a choice. It is also a path. Every choice that humans make takes them further along a path, either towards or away from evil. Doing evil can be a journey from minor incidents to massive evil.

During the Nuremberg Trials, a Nazi War Criminal told his American Judge, "I didn't know it would come to this". This was most likely a true statement. The American Judge told the Nazi war criminal on trial, "It came to this when the first innocent life was taken."

The lesson being that evil is a path. It can start on a small scale, and whoever is foolish enough to follow it, can end up somewhere they never intended to go. Conversely, each difficult decision made in favor of truth, humility, and justice takes that individual further away from evil incidents.

Most importantly, **all** species, not just humans, are deserving to be treated with justice, and without evil supremacy. The justification of human supremacy over other species as 'dominion' is simply an extension of human pride. The true meaning of dominion is not ownership and control, but rather stewardship and caretaking.

Can the banality of evil apply to evil human supremacy over other species?

Can a 'good' person purchase and drink cow's milk, every drop of which is preceded by violence and torture, and not be 'evil'?

Can a 'good' person not be 'evil' when he/she purchases and eats the flesh of another individual, albeit from another species, who has been tortured and murdered?

Can a 'good' person not be 'evil' when he/she purchases and eats or bakes with the unfertilized egg from the menstrual cycle of an individual who has been incarcerated all her life in a tiny prison with other imprisoned individuals, or locked in a warehouse the size of a football field with thousands of other unfortunate individuals?

Maybe the answers to these questions can be found in the results of these acts. Ecocide, causing the destruction of the planet, stems from human decisions – what to eat, what to wear, etc. The planet is dying from animal agriculture induced climate change; humans are dying from diet related non-communicable diseases; billions of sentient beings, whose care has been entrusted to humans through the original meaning of 'dominion', are dying. Can anything 'good' cause so much death? (Clue: the answer is 'No').

22

Akron, Ohio 1935

Is there a solution for supremacy, pride, lies, and destructive behavior? Yes, the solution is humility, gratitude, faith, self-inventory or examination of conscience, and making amends.

Almost 100 years ago, in the 1930's, a Wall Street entrepreneur traveled across the United States visiting companies listed on the stock exchange. He wanted first-hand, physical evidence to determine if these company's stocks were accurately priced, or under or over-valued.

This individual was Bill Wilson. When Bill W. arrived in Akron, Ohio, he used a public pay phone to seek help for a personal problem he was experiencing. A savvy Telephone Operator directed him to Dr. Bob.

The meeting between Bill W. and Dr. Bob started an initiative that is currently responsible for saving hundreds of thousands, and possibly millions, of human lives worldwide. Even the World Health Organization would have to admit that this program is one of the most, if not the most, successful health initiative in the history of the planet.

Bill W. and Dr. Bob both suffered from destructive alcoholism. Individuals afflicted with this, and other forms of addiction, typically use lies, deception, often theft of many kinds, and can be destructive to themselves, others and property. It can be deadly, and often is. These unfortunate individuals typically blame everyone and everything except themselves for their dilemma. They usually suffer from pride, dishonesty, destructive behavior, and lack of responsibility. These attributes could be considered evil and supremacist.

This is how Bill W. and Dr. Bob overcame potentially deadly alcoholism with a program, Alcoholism Anonymous, variations of which ultimately overcame many other deadly addictive illnesses around the world, saving hundreds of thousands, and possibly millions, of human lives.

There is a God! In this program, God is referred to as a 'Higher Power'. Human lives were saved by, among other things, turning their lives and wills over to the care of their Higher Power. This became a powerful, lifesaving force. It worked in most cases, only those individuals who could not, or would not, embrace this new lifestyle, were unsuccessful.

Individuals who were willing to try, turned their spiritual lives around from willful and prideful ones, to lives of humility, gratitude, faith, and responsibility, and in the process saved their physical lives. This inspirational twelve-step program, originally conceived to overcome Alcoholism, was later expanded to include almost every conceivable human situation and is credited with saving countless lives all around the world.

Unfortunately, there is a dark side to the human experience, another force, the fruits of which are often called the Deadly or Capital Sins. These are: pride, envy, gluttony, greed, lust, sloth, and anger. Pride is considered the deadliest of all the deadly sins because it is responsible for misery, death, destruction, and is the root of supremacy. C.S. Lewis says pride is the complete anti-God state of mind. Supremacy, an insidious form of pride, is ultimately responsible for the on-going unsustainable treatment of this planet, and all life on it.

Pride starts by convincing individuals that they are better than others, and that they are entitled to everything for their own use, such as other humans, other species, and natural resources. Pride/Supremacy go on to convince individuals that their needs are more important than the needs of others, and that others – humans, other species, and nature have no rights that supersede their human rights. In its severest form, pride holds that all others deserve nothing.

Pride and supremacy rationalize that taking what an individual wants, regardless of how it affects others, is not only acceptable, but an entitlement. We see the results of pride and supremacy in the way some humans treat other humans, other species, and the non- renewable resources on our precious, dying planet Earth. Humility, honesty and faith are the antidotes to the destructive forces of pride, undisputedly the underlying cause of supremacy, which is destroying other species, natural resources, and the entire planet.

The simple solution to global warming, pollution, species extinction, deforestation, desertification, anti-microbial resistance, non-communicable diseases, zoonotic disease and other sustainability issues is to overcome destructive pride and supremacy with life-saving humility, gratitude, and making amends! It is only when the humans recognize this concept and embrace it that we will ever move beyond the Anthropocene Epoch.

Part Three

The Solution: Legislation

23

The Need For
Environmental Law

Transformative change from the destructive path the Earth is on now demands immediate attention and solid support for initiatives and advances in Earth-Centered Law and Ecological Economics.

Environmental laws have failed to effectively address climate change, reduce pollution or prevent species extinction and habitat loss. Recognizing the rights of all of Nature in enforceable laws fills that void and is complementary to human rights.

The human right to a sustainable healthy environment cannot be achieved without first securing Nature's rights. Further, the human right to life is meaningless if the ecosystems that sustain humankind do not also have the legal rights to exist.

The first step in creating rights for Nature is the recognition that non-human animals are sentient beings, not mere property, and must be afforded respect and legal recognition. This recognition is growing around the world, particularly for those animals most easily appreciated by humans, their companion pets. However, farmed and other exploited animals are just as intelligent and affectionate as companion animals, and no less deserving of enforceable rights.

The key to sustainability and to assure a healthy planet lies in restoring humanity's broken relationship with the land, other sentient beings, and with Nature as a whole. This can only be achieved in a way that is mandatory and not optional.

24

Earth Centered Law

Without a radical change in direction the Earth is going, inevitable destruction of the planet will eventually occur. Earth-Centered Laws are the solution to the problem.

Currently in the world today there are initiatives which strive to give nature rights. These are commonly known as Earth Centered Laws. Earth Centered Laws are non-anthropocentric. They grant moral standing and enforceable rights to nature and all sentient beings. Animals, birds, plants, water, landscapes, and more are legally protected.

Any account of morality that has the effect of removing humans from the position of supremacy is non-anthropocentric.

Earth Centered Laws involve the recognition that the universe and its Creator are the source of the fundamental rights of all members of the Earth community, human and non-human, rather than rights being some part of the human governance system. Accordingly, these rights cannot be validly circumscribed or abrogated by human jurisprudence.

Earth-Centered Laws are a means of recognizing the rights of the non-human members of the Earth community, and a means of restraining humans from unjustifiably preventing non-humans from fulfilling those rights. Earth-Centered Law is rooted in the idea that other sentient beings, nature and ecosystems have the right to exist, thrive, and evolve. Most importantly, all of nature should be able to pursue and defend its rights in court, just like people can.

This concept is predicated on humanity accepting the stark reality that its well-being is derived from the well-being of the Earth, and that to sustain all life on the planet, and guarantee future generations of all species, it is necessary to live in harmony with Nature and be guided by the enforceable Earth-Centered Laws.

Values advanced by that paradigm, such as equity, cooperation, dialogue, inclusion, comprehension, agreement, respect and mutual inspiration are necessary in the journey to move beyond the Anthropocene Epoch. These values contrast sharply with profitability and the current growth-based economic system. Recognizing Nature as a subject of law contrasts sharply with current environmental protection laws, which are anthropocentric.

A fundamental reason for the lack of effectiveness of environmental law in protecting Nature can be attributed to the fact that it never replaced the idea of the endless exploitation of the planet with the concept of equal justice for all, and sustainability. The weakness of environmental law is directly linked to the fact that it stops at anthropocentric private law.

Despite decades of environmental legislation, Earth's health continues to decline. Because our current laws protect Nature only for the benefit of people and corporations, profit usually takes priority over Nature. Even when environmental issues are brought to court, people must prove that the environmental damage violates their own rights since the environment has no rights of its own.

Environmental laws have failed to reduce pollution, prevent species extinction and habitat loss, and curtail global warming. Recognizing the rights of Nature in law fills the existing void and proves complementary to human rights.

Traditional knowledge and customary laws of indigenous peoples embody respect for other sentient beings, and an understanding that human governance systems must be derived from the laws of the Earth. This is exemplified where there is respect and recognition of indigenous ancestral lands, sacred natural sites, knowledge and practices, enabling communities to continue to live in harmony with the landscape and wildlife as they have for generations.

There has been growing recognition of the customary laws of indigenous peoples in national constitutions and international law. Government policies, from the local to the national levels, have added to advancements in recognizing the contribution of customary governance systems to living in harmony with Nature. Traditional indigenous food systems also demonstrate an interdependent sociocultural relationship with Mother Earth, in contrast with the globalized corporate food system, which disconnects food consumption from food production.

Recent studies have revealed a strong correlation between the density of organizations and networks promoting the rights of Nature and countries where legal provisions on the rights of Nature are emerging. This indicates a mainstreaming of the concept of the rights of Nature and the building of partnerships with organizations and movements whose activities are aligned with the rights of Nature.

The Earth-Centered way of living involving scientists, activists and indigenous peoples, who have decried the escalating destruction of Earth's natural system for decades, is a powerful global movement. People confronted with climate change and biodiversity loss of unimaginable scale are creating a growing rights-based movement for Nature.

The emergency responses to environmental crisis have demonstrated the ability of some Governments to act decisively when the stakes are high enough. This indicates a capacity for making deep-seated structural change when considered necessary.

The human right to life is meaningless if the ecosystems that sustain humans do not also have the legal rights to exist. With the acceleration of climate change and ecosystems being pushed to collapse, the human right to a healthy environment cannot be achieved without first securing Nature's own rights.

The worldviews and cosmogonies, traditional knowledge and customary laws of indigenous peoples, also embody that respect for other sentient beings, and an understanding that human governance systems must be derived from the laws of the Earth. This is exemplified where there is respect and recognition of indigenous ancestral lands, sacred natural sites, knowledge and practices, enabling communities to continue to live in harmony with the landscape and wildlife as they have for generations.

It is heartening that initiatives resonate globally with the call for a peaceful, virtuous, and harmonious coexistence between humans, nature, and all the sentient beings who share the planet.

25

Earth Jurisprudence

Earth jurisprudence is a philosophy and practice through which humanity accepts the reality that its well-being is derived from the well-being of the Earth, and to sustain all life on the planet and guarantee future generations of all species, it is necessary to live in harmony with Nature, and be guided by the laws of the Earth.

Earth jurisprudence is a philosophy of law and human governance that is based on the fact that humans are only one part of a wider community of beings and that the welfare of each member of that community is dependent on the welfare of the Earth as a whole. It states that human societies will be viable and flourish only if they regulate themselves as part of this wider Earth community and do so in a way that is consistent with the fundamental laws or principles that govern how the universe functions, which is the 'Great Jurisprudence'.

Earth jurisprudence seeks to expand understanding of the relevance of governance beyond humanity to the whole Earth community. It is Earth-centric rather than anthropocentric. It is concerned with the maintenance and regulation of relations between all members of the Earth community, not just between human beings. Earth jurisprudence is intended to provide a philosophical basis for the development and implementation of human governance systems, which may include ethics, laws, institutions, policies and practices. It also places an emphasis on the internalization of these insights and on personal practice, in living in accordance with Earth jurisprudence as a way of life.

Earth jurisprudence can be differentiated from the Great jurisprudence, but it can also be understood as being embedded within it. Earth jurisprudence can be seen as a special case of the Great jurisprudence, applying universal principles to the governmental, societal and biological processes of Earth.

The need for a new jurisprudence was first identified by Thomas Berry who identified the destructive anthropocentrism on which existing legal and political structures are based as a major impediment to the necessary transition to an ecological age in which humans would seek a new intimacy with the integral functioning of the natural world.

Earth jurisprudence should reflect a particular human community's understanding of how to regulate itself as part of the Earth community and should express the qualities of the Great jurisprudence of which it is part. The specific applications of Earth jurisprudence will vary from society to society but shares common elements.

These elements include: a recognition that any Earth jurisprudence exists within a wider context that shapes it and influences how it functions; a recognition that the universe is the source of the fundamental 'Earth rights' of all members of the Earth community, rather than some part of the human governance system and accordingly these rights cannot be validly circumscribed or abrogated by human jurisprudence; a means of recognizing the roles and 'rights' of non-human members of the Earth community and of restraining humans from unjustifiably preventing them fulfilling those roles; a concern for reciprocity and the maintenance of a dynamic equilibrium between all the members of the Earth community determined by what is best for the system as a whole (Earth justice); and an approach to condoning or disapproving human conduct on the basis of whether or not the conduct strengthens or weakens the bonds that constitute the Earth community.

Over the past decade, Earth Jurisprudence has been gaining ground in an increasing number of United Nations Member States. Through the philosophy and practice of Earth jurisprudence, humanity accepts the reality that its well-being is derived from the well-being of the Earth and that, to sustain all life on the planet and guarantee future generations of all species, it is necessary to live in harmony with Nature. Most importantly, jurisprudence needs to move from an Anthropocene focus, become more enlightened, and include planet Earth, all of the species, and all of Nature in enforceable laws.

26

Earth Economics

Ecological economics seeks to ground economic thinking and practice in physical reality. Its goal is the improvement of human well-being through development. It seeks to ensure this achievement through planning the sustainable development of both ecosystems and societies. Understandably, there is some controversy between the terms: development and sustainable development.

It is Earth-Centered, as opposed to being Anthropocentric. Ecological Economics, from an Earth jurisprudence perspective, would be an economic framework that is holistic, values based, and Earth-Centered. That is - all parts of Nature are considered subjects rather than objects. Ecological Economics strives to achieve the prosperity and flourishment of all living and non-living things, rather than just focusing on the material prosperity of humans at the expense of other species and Nature.

Ecological economics is distinguished from neoclassical economics by its assertion that the economy is embedded within an environmental system. Ecology deals with the energy and matter transactions of life and of the Earth itself. The human economy is contained within this system. Ecological economists argue that neoclassical economics has ignored the environment entirely, or at best, considers it to be a part of the human economy.

Ecological economics makes the distinction between growth, quantitative increase in economic output, and development, qualitative improvement of the quality of life. There has been a move to regard ecosystems functions as goods and services. This is controversial due to the possibility of focusing on values found in mainstream economics, and the danger of regarding Nature as a commodity. This has been referred to as 'selling out on Nature'.

Ecological economists point out that beyond modest levels, increased per-capita consumption, which is the typical economic measure of 'standard of living' may not always lead to improvements in human well-being. It may have harmful effects on the environment and broader social well-being. This situation is sometimes referred to as uneconomic growth. Ecological economics challenges the conventional approach towards natural resources, claiming that it undervalues natural capital by considering it interchangeable with human-made capital—labor and technology.

The sustainability view argues that natural resources and ecological functions are irreplaceable, and that economic policy has a fiduciary responsibility to the greater ecological world. Sustainable development must take a different approach to valuing natural resources and ecological functions.

Ecological economics rejects the current view of energy economics. Specifically, that growth in energy supply is related to well-being, and focuses instead on biodiversity and creativity. This is referred to as natural capital and individual capital in terminology used to describe them economically.

Ecological economics focuses primarily on the key issues of uneconomic growth and quality of life. Ecological economists are inclined to acknowledge that much of what is important in human well-being is not analyzable from a strictly economic standpoint and suggests that an interdisciplinary approach combining social and natural sciences be used to address this.

Ecological economists maintain that ecosystems produce enormous flows of goods and services for humans. However, there is intense debate regarding how and when to place values on these benefits. Treating ecosystems as goods and services to be valued in monetary terms is itself controversial. A common objection is that life is precious or priceless, and that this degrades to it being worthless in cost-benefit analysis and other standard economic methods.

Ecological economics based on Earth jurisprudence attributes 'humane' value to non-living things as well as all living things.

Nature, including all aspects of planet Earth, is given the same consideration as human beings. Unlike the current Gross Domestic Product (GDP) based economic framework that considers non-living things as 'dead' and thus 'less important and less valuable', Ecological economics would ensure the safety, security, prosperity, and flourishment of all of planet Earth.

Ecological economics maintains that it is possible to work with, and live in, a relationship with Nature in a harmonious way, while at the same time achieving development and progress.

27

United Nations
Harmony with Nature

Despite warnings of unsustainable development since the 1960s, backed by evidence from scientists about concentrations of greenhouse gas emissions, deforestation and species extinction in reference to production and consumption causing a sixth mass extinction, the loss of biodiversity from terrestrial and aquatic ecosystems continues to increase at rates unprecedented in human history.

For the past decade, the United Nations Harmony With Nature Program has documented and analyzed legislation and policies on the rights of Nature that have been either adopted or for which work is currently ongoing in 35 countries and it analyzed the core tenets of those important contributions.

The Program has also documented and analyzed collaboration among Non-Governmental Organizations (NGOs), civil society organizations, legislators, and legislative bodies working together to draft, adopt and implement laws or policies recognizing Nature as a subject of rights and/or a legal "person", protected by law.

The Harmony With Nature Program commends all efforts to develop and implement alternatives to the dominant growth-insistent economic model, and to capture lessons from the present to develop regenerative systems. The Program emphasizes the need for imagining and creating a new normalcy that prioritizes planetary health and well-being for all.

The cases and developments in Ecological economics and Earth-Centered Law presented in the report reveal promise and potential to protect the planet and all its inhabitants. Those countries around the world whose non-anthropocentric decisions, laws and policies are at the forefront of this are responsible for this change in direction.

On December 19, 2019, the United Nations General Assembly adopted resolution 74/224, its eleventh resolution on Harmony with Nature, by which it requested the President of the General Assembly to convene, at its seventy-fourth session, an interactive dialogue in commemoration of International Mother Earth Day on 22 April 2020, with the participation of Member States, United Nations organizations, independent experts and other stakeholders.

Then, in a statement commemorating International Mother Earth Day, 2020, the United Nations Secretary General stressed that, while all eyes were on the COVID-19 pandemic, there was another life-threatening emergency: the planet's unfolding environmental crisis. He emphasized that biodiversity was in steep decline, that climate disruption was approaching a point of no return, that the pandemic was an unprecedented wake-up call, and that recovery must be viewed as a real opportunity to do things right for the future.

On International Mother Earth Day, 22 April 2021, the President of the United Nations General Assembly delivered a statement in which he emphasized that: Mother Earth would only be preserved "through a paradigm shift from a human-centric society to an Earth-centered global ecosystem." In other words, to survive, the planet needs to go beyond the Anthropocene Epoch.

28

Nations With
Earth Centered Laws

Around the world, there have been initiatives which seek to give rights to Nature. These are a few, and hopefully there will be more in the future.

On November 7, 2019, the Constitutional Court of Guatemala rendered a verdict recognizing the spiritual and cultural relationship between indigenous people and the water element, recognizing water as a living entity. In the verdict, it was noted that the agrarian transformation and mining laws of Guatemala excluded the sacred character that water possessed and the possibility that water was a living being, a subject that merited having rights, and therefore could not be killed by contamination. It was also noted that water was a living entity with cycles, that connected it with the cosmos and that it was a nahual, guardian spirit, for the Maya people.

Ecuador has enforceable non-human rights in its Constitution. In 2008, Ecuador became the first nation to grant constitutional Rights for Nature, or Pachamama, as Mother Earth is known, in the cosmovision of the Quechua people living in the Andes. The Rights for Nature acknowledges that nature in all its forms has the right to exist, persist, maintain, and regenerate its vital cycles, and that people have the legal authority to enforce these rights on behalf of all ecosystems.

Ecuador indicated that, given the current uncertain times, it was of the utmost relevance for countries and people around the world to reflect on the importance of a harmonious relationship between human beings and Nature. Additionally, Ecuador maintains that harmony with Nature is intrinsic to the achievement of sustainable development and is also in line with global efforts to protect biodiversity, change consumption and production patterns, combat the adverse effects of climate change, end plastic pollution, build resilient communities, and reduce inequalities for current and future generations.

In its statement, Ecuador underscored that the COVID-19 pandemic was linked to the poor health of ecosystems and specifically the abuse and illegal trade of wildlife and emphasized that the exercise of human rights depended on biodiversity conservation. Ecuador expressed confidence that, once the current pandemic situation had passed, the interactive dialogues would continue, as would the sharing of good practices on harmony with Nature within the United Nations.

The Plurinational State of Bolivia recognized in its Constitution of 2009, the principles of 'buen vivir' (good living) for guiding State action. This includes everyone – of all species.

Argentina made history in 2022 with a salmon farming ban. The new law halted plans to build an intensive salmon farm on Argentina's south coast. It also prohibits "all salmon farming and production activities" due to serious concerns about sustainability. This makes Argentina the first country to ban open net salmon farming. Law makers unanimously approved the bill to ban all salmon fishing. It is the first of its kind in the world, but hopefully not the last. The salmon industry is notorious for environmental disasters and harm to ecosystems, not to mention its impact on the welfare of the fish. The horrific conditions of fish farms cause diseases to incarcerated fish and spill-over adversely affects wild fish. The antibiotics used to combat these horrific conditions enter surrounding waters and ultimately cause antibiotic resistance in both wild marine life and in humans.

Argentina held the First International Virtual Congress on Animal Law, in May 2020. The Congress had an audience of close to

2,000 participants, and speakers from more than 40 countries.

In Uganda, on November 22, 2019, the Buliisa District Local Government Council passed a Resolution expressing concern for Mother Earth and all species on Earth, and that the Council has a responsibility to protect the well-being of the planet. The customary laws of the Bagungu custodian clans note "the concern of the Bagungu clan leaders for Butoka, Mother Earth, and for the future generations of all species of the Earth" and there is an "ancestral responsibility to protect the well-being of their land, and of the planet".

Benin, Kenya and Zimbabwe have African Earth jurisprudence practitioners and the Gaia Foundation who are facilitating similar progress in creating and recognizing rights for nature and all species.

Vanuatu, a small island nation with an archipelago of about 80 islands, has a Stop Ecocide initiative. President Nikenike Vurobaravu of Vanuatu has called for

United Nations member states to include the crime of ecocide in in the Rome Statute of the International Criminal Court. President Vurobaravu told the UN General Assembly " acting with knowledge of severe and widespread or long term damage to the environment can no longer be tolerated."

Independent State of Samoa, People's Republic of Bangladesh, Belgium and Finland have also expressed support for the ecocide conversation at the International Criminal Court

United Kingdom Shadow Foreign Secretary David Lammy, pledged UK's Labor Party's support for a new international law of ecocide. Lammy stated that "we will seek to work with allies and partners to create a new international law of ecocide to criminalize the wanton and widespread destruction of the environment."

The United Nations Harmony with Nature program has documented and analyzed legislation and policies on the Rights of Nature that have been either adopted or are currently being worked on in 35 countries. In addition, the United Nations General Assembly proclaimed April 22 as International Mother Earth Day and adopted its first Resolution on Harmony with Nature.

These forward thinking, non-anthropocentric countries are the front-runners in impacting law and policy around the world, and hopefully the harbingers of a planet that is no longer dominated by the destructiveness of human supremacy.

29

The Last Frontier:
A UN Convention Against
Speciesism

"Non-human animals are sentient beings, not mere property, and they must be afforded respect and legal recognition." United Nations Secretary General Antonio Guterres.

Speciesism is a crime which should be recognized under international law. It is contrary to the spirit and aims of the United Nations and should be condemned by the civilized world. It should be recognized that in all periods of history speciesism has inflicted great losses on individuals and the planet, and that the world needs to be liberated from such an odious scourge.

Speciesism causes epidemics, pandemics, some Non-Communicable Diseases (NCDs), as well as many other health issues, environmental issues including climate change, air, water and land pollution, misuse of scarce resources. It is the leading cause of habit destruction, species extinction, biodiversity loss, and is the direct result of the abuse and exploitation of other species for the benefit of the human species.

The purpose of the United Nations Convention Against Speciesism is not only to give enforceable rights to members of all species beyond the human species, but also to recognize that members of all species are sentient beings and not property, and that they are entitled to live in peace without exploitation of any kind by any other species, specifically humans.

A United Nations Convention Against Speciesism is the single most import and political solution which will ensure global health and sustainability for all inhabitants of planet Earth, as well as for the Earth itself. It would give all sentient beings enforceable rights, which is the next step on the journey to move beyond the Anthropocene Epoch.

A United Nations Convention Against Speciesism would promote and protect the rights of all species. This Convention would be an internationally recognized instrument for the protection of all inhabitants of Earth. Currently, there are no universally recognized rights or protection afforded to the most vulnerable on the planet, or to the planet itself.

A United Nations Convention Against Speciesism is a logical progression following all previous United Nations Conventions. This includes the end of World War II United Nations Convention Against Genocide in 1948, the United Nations Convention Against Torture in 1984, the United Nations Convention on the Elimination of all forms of Discrimination Against Women (CEDAW) in 1979, and the United Nations Convention on the Rights of the Child in 1989.

Speciesism, the exploitation, and violent abuse of individuals of another species, is not recognized as a category of discrimination, and is widely tolerated throughout the world. Species other than humans are excluded from any protection, are treated as objects instead of rights holders, and are subjected to violence and abuse of all kinds. Respect for the rights of all species benefits everyone: humans, those of other species, and the planet.

The United Nations recommendation of stricter regulations of live markets, the UN Universal Declaration of Animal Welfare, global investigations, and national and local laws and regulations have not been effective in solving the problem. What is needed is a radical, comprehensive approach. Vegan International is advocating a United Nations Convention Against Speciesism to effectively resolve this issue and give enforceable rights to all in order to end the destructive path we are currently on and set the course for a healthier, more equitable future, by addressing the most destructive

health and environmental problem:
Speciesism.

Animals are the least protected and most
exploited individuals on the planet – a planet
that is currently on a trajectory headed for
disaster if radical changes are not
implemented. Everyone deserves justice,
and a United Nations 'Place at the table'
regardless of species. 'No one left behind',
should apply to everyone on planet Earth,
not just to one species. There needs to be a
radical, comprehensive approach to provide
justice for all inhabitants of planet Earth.

Current environmental laws have failed to
reduce pollution, prevent biodiversity loss,
species extinction, and habitat loss.
Recognizing the rights of Nature, and
especially of all species, in a comprehensive,
enforceable law - a United Nations
Convention Against Speciesism - fills that
void and is necessary for the survival of the
planet.

A United Nations Convention is needed to promote and protect the rights of all species. This Convention would be an internationally recognized instrument for the protection of all inhabitants of Earth. Currently, there are no rights or protection afforded to the most vulnerable on the planet, or to the planet itself.

This proposed Convention would be an internationally recognized instrument for the protection of all inhabitants of Earth. Speciesism, the exploitation, and abuse of individuals of other species, is not recognized as a category of discrimination, and is widely tolerated throughout the world. Species other than humans are excluded from any protection, are treated as objects instead of rights holders, and are subjected to violence and abuse of all kinds. Respect for the rights of all species benefits everyone: humans, those of other species, and the planet.

A United Nations Convention Against Speciesism is a simple solution to reduce climate change, reduce hunger, achieve food security, improve global health, reduce poverty, achieve food security, improve nutrition, promote sustainable consumption, promote sustainable veganic agriculture, reduce human mortality and morbidity from zoonotic and diet related disease such as heart disease, diabetes, and some cancers, sustainably manage the scarce resources of land and water, combat climate change, sustainably manage forests, and curtail pollution of air, water, and land, species extinction, habitat destruction, and give justice to billions of unjustly incarcerated and exploited individuals.

The benefits of the proposed United Nations Convention Against Speciesism include preventing or eliminating zoonotic disease. Most epidemics and pandemics and serious infectious diseases are zoonotic - caused by exploitation of animals by humans. This includes Covid-19, HIV, SARS, MERS, Swine Flu, Avian Flu, and the deadliest diseases in history – Black Death, HIV, and Spanish Flu. A pathogen jumps from exploited, abused, often unjustly incarcerated animals to humans, and is then transmitted directly among humans.

Eliminating speciesism would reduce human mortality and morbidity. There is copious documentation that transitioning from the fat and cholesterol filled meat and dairy based diet to a fiber rich plant-based diet can eliminate heart disease, cancer, diabetes and antibiotic resistance.

Other benefits include halting or reversing climate change. Scientific facts prove that the main cause of global warming melting polar ice caps and raising sea water levels is methane. Methane traps heat in the atmosphere more effectively than carbon dioxide. Methane from the digestive systems of animals raised for the meat and dairy based diet is directly responsible for this impending disaster.

Additionally, land used to grow crops to feed animals unjustly murdered for food, could be used to grow crops to feed hungry and starving human children and adults.

This would significantly reduce world hunger especially in developing nations which export crops while they and their own children are starving.

Air, water, and land pollution is a direct result of animal agriculture. In the United States, animal agriculture produces more pollution than all other industries combined. An enforceable Convention ratified by the US could end this.

The scarce resources of land and water are being used unsustainably. Rainforests are cut and burned down to provide grazing land, and land and to grow crops to feed to animals raised for food. It takes a hundred times more water to produce meat than vegetables. This proposed Convention could make that unnecessary.

Species extinction and habitat destruction are a direct result of Speciesism. As animal agriculture grows, it needs more and more resources of land and water, destroying the habitats of existing species and causing extinction of irreplaceable individuals. This loss of biodiversity is a contributing factor in zoonotic disease and could end with the proposed Convention.

Eliminating Speciesism with an enforceable United Nations Convention would help to achieve the Sustainable Development Goals by ultimately reducing poverty, achieving food security, improving nutrition, promoting sustainable consumption, promoting sustainable veganic agriculture, reducing human mortality and morbidity from zoonotic disease and diet related disease such as heart disease, diabetes, and cancer, sustainably managing the scarce resources of land and water, combating climate change, sustainably managing forests, and reducing pollution of air, water, and land.

A shift to the plant-based diet, and giving animals universal rights, would promote sustainability, and remove the specter of pandemic zoonotic disease. Animals, birds and fish are the least protected, most exploited individuals on a planet that is currently headed for disaster if radical changes are not implemented. These individuals are our co-inhabitants on planet Earth.

United Nations Sustainable Development Goal 16 'Peace and Justice' currently does not include all individuals on Earth. It is only applied to the human species. This outrageous injustice threatens the very existence of human life through zoonotic pandemics, and other serious health issues, as well as threatens the destruction of planet Earth through methane induced climate change, biodiversity loss, and species extinction. These unfortunate forgotten non-human individuals are in need of justice.

The United Nations Convention Against Speciesism proposed by Vegan International would bring clarity to the nature of the rights of all species and to the responsibilities necessary to protect them. It would view all species as rights-holders, and these rights would be in a single document. In addition, the proposed Convention would raise public awareness in those nations which do not ratify it.

A United Nations Convention Against Speciesism finally 'leaves no one behind'. It creates a 'place at the table' for all inhabitants of planet Earth. It is a simple solution to reduce climate change, reduce hunger, achieve food security, improve nutrition and human health by reducing human mortality and morbidity from diet related disease such as heart disease, diabetes, and some cancers, reduce poverty, promote sustainable consumption, promote sustainable veganic agriculture, sustainably manage the scarce resources of land and water, sustainably manage forests, reducing water, air and land pollution, improve sanitation, and achieve justice for all inhabitants of planet Earth.

This is only a first step. It is a paradigm shift from the path to destruction the Earth is currently on, to a move towards sustainability based on justice for all. This new direction will involve other responsible actions such as giving rights to nature, water, land, and a measure of human success based not on financial parameters, but on intrinsic values including justice, respect, concern, co-operation and happiness.

30

Conclusion

The current Anthropocene Epoch is characterized by one species, humans, dominating all other species, and destroying planet Earth. Human society has become so powerful that it affects the fate of the entire biosphere. Unfortunately, this has not been accompanied by the necessary responsibility, foresight, accountability, or justice to create or maintain sustainability. Without a radical change in the direction the Earth is going, inevitable destruction of the planet will eventually occur.

This heedless dominion over the Earth is simply not sustainable. Feeding much of the world's edible grain crop to unjustly incarcerated farmed individuals while vulnerable humans starve or are malnourished is not only inexcusable injustice but is a grossly inefficient and unsustainable use of natural resources, simultaneously creating mounting human health, pollution, and global warming problems.

Speciesism is foremost a justice issue. It is unjust, unsustainable, and destructive. It is treating animals as slaves of humans. The unfortunate individuals, who are eaten, used for clothing, experiments, and entertainment, have no rights of their own. As we all know from the past, individuals kidnapped in Africa, and forced to be slaves elsewhere, did not want to be treated better, they wanted to be free and have rights. All species share those same feelings and desires - to raise their families in peace, and be free to live a normal, natural life.

Justice belongs to everyone on planet Earth, not just those who can enforce it with power and money. Justice for all species is a primary factor in the move away from the Anthropocene Epoch, and away from the destruction of planet Earth.

Giving rights to members of all species is a simple solution to reduce climate change, achieve food security, improve nutrition and human health by reducing diet related disease such as heart disease, diabetes, and cancer, reduce human hunger and poverty, sustainably manage the scarce resources of land and water, sustainably manage forests, reduce water, air and land pollution, and most importantly, to achieve justice for all inhabitants of planet Earth.

Throughout its 75-year history, the United Nations has attempted to give a voice to the voiceless. Until recently this voice has been limited to the members of the human species. One of the goals of the United Nations is to give all humans a 'place at the table' and that no human should be 'left behind'. Nowhere does it mention members of other species, the environment, water, land, nature, or anything other than humans. The United Nations itself needs to move beyond the Anthropocene Epoch.

Responsibility now lies with the United Nations and individual nations to be champions of non-anthropocentrism, a voice on behalf of the natural world, and to play leading roles for a twenty-first century global Earth-Centered transition, in which the lives of all humans and non-human matter.

This giant step forward would mark the beginning of the end of the Anthropocene Epoch, and the day that the Earth moves in a sustainable path which includes justice for all species, not just the human species.

Only when pride is superseded by compassion for all species, and all species are given enforceable rights, will planet Earth become truly sustainable, and move beyond the Anthropocene Epoch!

Liberty 61 Books

Liberty 61 Books is a specialty Publisher focusing on Non-Fiction topics including: Health, Science, Biography, Travel, Inspiration, Peace, Justice, and other relevant topics.

Liberty 61 Books is dedicated to the concept of Justice, and founded on the Biblical verse in Isaiah Chapter 61: "Creator God brings Liberty to the Captives, and sets the Prisoners free."

"The Lord God Loves Justice"

Sharon Leontine Wallenberg

Sharon Leontine Wallenberg is the Author of:

"The Search for Raoul Wallenberg - The Truth",

"A Plant-Based Lifestyle For You And The Planet",

"Where Do You Get Your Protein - Rethinking Food",

and Founder of:

Vegan International
a 501c3 Not-For-Profit,
United Nations Economic and
Social Council (ECOSOC)
Non-Governmental Organization
(NGO) applicant.